UNMASKING PROPHETIC BIAS

The Politicization of the American Prophetic Movement

Eddie Massey III

CONTENTS

INTRODUCTION: PITFALLS IN THE AMERICAN PROPHETIC MOVEMENT

God has graced the 21st century church with a great restoration of key fivefold offices. While many churches still operate on a two-fold system built around the offices of the pastor and teacher, there are several that have embraced the New Testament five-fold apostolic framework. The revelatory offices of the apostle and prophet have seen a great increase in recent decades. The restoration of these key ministry gifts have birthed a profound level of revelatory and prophetic acumen that has brought the body of Christ light-years ahead in many respects.

One consequence in particular is also the restoration of the 1 Corinthians 14 gift of prophecy that Paul says is used for edification, exhortation, and comfort. Many believers who do not occupy the office of prophet have been able to move in the 1 Corinthians 14 gift, bringing transformation in the lives of countless souls globally.

Prophetic evangelism is being used to destroy strongholds, heal the sick, and demonstrate God's power and love in profound ways. However, as the old adage goes, "with great power, comes great responsibility." There has been a profound level of error associated with the modern prophetic movement.

Limited not only to erroneous prophecies, but to heart wrenching theological errors and even heretical teachings. The prophetic movement has been associated with significant issues that need to be addressed in a comprehensive and biblically sound manner if we're to have any significant progress in advancing Heaven's agenda on Earth.

Recent events in particular have highlighted serious concerns that threaten the future of our collective stewardship of Christ's gift to the church. The partisan political climate of the United States and the COVID-19 pandemic have highlighted biblically immature, theologically ignorant, and presumptuous behavior in many of those who claim to be speaking on behalf of the Spirit of God.

Many I believe truly love God and are eager to be used by him, but like the Apostle Paul said in Romans 10:2, "For I bear them witness that they have a zeal for God, but not according to knowledge."

In the Old Testament, prophets anointed kings and the kingdoms of the Earth shook, because of the prophetic utterances that came from God's mouthpieces. Today, there seems to be an entirely different dynamic going on in the prophetic movement in America.

The evangelical alignment with the political right in the United States has created an ungodly union between the prophetic office and the conservative agenda. Instead of prophets speaking on behalf of God. We now see prophets speaking on behalf of their preferred political party.

The church believes that the agenda of the political right is the agenda of heaven. Furthermore they've been indoctrinated to believe that God believes in American exceptionalism. In reality,

American is a nation that must repent just like any other. God is not committed to the American dream, he's committed to his will. Many prominent prophetic voices have become spokesmen for American geopolitical interests and policies that Heaven is about to bring judgement against throughout the 21st century.

Once God's prophet is more in tune to the voice of the earthly kings than to the King of Kings, their bias will masquerade as the voice of God for a generation and for a people. While I love America, my nation, and my people we must be objective to properly discern the will, purpose and plan of God. There are impending judgements coming that many prophets are silent about because of their personal biases.

ARE YOU REALLY VOTING YOUR FAITH?

You just left the polls with a great feeling of accomplishment because you did God a big favor. You voted straight ticket republican because they obviously have God's plan for the nation in mind. They have Christian values, like being pro-life. Unlike those godless liberals who have forgotten God and are bringing this nation to hell. After all if Biden is elected "people will be having sex with animals."[i] Now that you've done your part in helping God get his chosen people in office, your conscience can be clear. Now, you can pat yourself on the back and thank God that you're not one of those satanic leftist liberals like AOC.

Next time you go and pray you can be just like one of Jesus' favorite Pharisees in Luke 18:11. "God, I thank you that I am not like other men, extortioners, unjust, adulterers, or even like this tax collector" or even that godless liberal pro-choice Democrat that's filled with the Antichrist agenda.

The problem here is that the concept of defining your biblical faith that was developed over thousands of years and on the blood of numerous martyrs on a single issue is extremely limiting. It's also very limiting to define your faith to political matters that often prey on the circumstances and biases of the populous to advance personal or party agendas.

Let's take a popular example, abortion. A popular line of reasoning for voting your faith is the following logical syllogism.

1. Violating the sanctity of life is a sin
2. Abortion unjustly ends human life
3. Therefore abortion is a sin

Most religious conservatives find common ground in the above logic, yet don't define voting their faith by the loss of life incurred by voting for the same candidates due to other policies. Voting for any modern president would also violate the sanctity of human life by nature of how America built and maintains its status a global superpower.

If we apply the same line of reason to a myriad of domestic and foreign policy issues that the current and past presidential administrations have had to deal with, we can see that both democrat and republican presidents have directly enacted policies that desecrate the value of human life.

Post-WWII US Presidents on both sides of the isle have both committed unspeakable atrocities. Even, the patron saint of the conservative movement, Ronald Regan, was carried away in their dissimulation.

The Regan administration gave direct support to the Guatemalan military as it executed a brutal genocide operation against indigenous groups in Guatemala which at least 200,000 people were either killed or disappeared.

Of which an alarming number of children were "the direct victims of arbitrary execution, forced disappearance, torture, rape and other violations of their fundamental rights."[ii] Reagan's rap sheet of international war crimes even includes being convicted by the International Court of Justice. Despite being guilty of brutal murders of innocent people all throughout the world, US of course, exempted themselves from international court oversight.[iii]

War crimes are certainly not limited to the Republican Party nor the 20th century. President Obama's lamentable and inhumane drone policy has harmed an innumerable number of civilians. Drone strikes are often thought of for being precise. In an address at the National Defense University President Obama claimed that "before any strike is taken, there must be near-certainty that no civilians will be killed or injured -- the highest standard we can set."[iv]

However that rhetoric is far from true. Drones under the Obama administration were found to be ten times more likely to kill civilians than manned aerial operations.[v] Furthermore, the administration employed double-tap tactics to incite fear. In other words after successfully striking a target, another drone strike would occur killing civilian first responders who were often heading to rescue other civilians that were harmed in the first strike.[vi]

The sanctity of life abroad has fared no better under the Trump administration. In fact President Trump has expanded several of President Obama's most controversial military policies. Under the Trump administration there has been a 215% increase in civilian deaths in foreign operations.[vii]

As civilian deaths abroad continue to rise, the Trump administration has taken great effort to end civilian casualty reporting requirements.[viii] Despite supplying weapons for Saudi Arabia's Dahyan air strike in which a civilian school bus was bombed killing over 40 children[ix]. Oddly enough, Saudi Arabia called the indiscriminate bombing of children under the age of 10, a "legitimate military operation."[x]

Despite blowing up a school bus and other mass casualty events, the Trump administration continues to fund the conflict. I wonder if the school children who were blown up would think that the Trump administration is pro-life if they were alive today.

If I had the time, we could examine several specific instances under democrat and republican administrations where the sanctity of life has been violated. From the deaths of innocent children to the overthrow of democratic leaders in support of authoritarian ones for the sake of US goals, there is no "holy" party in the US two party system.

For we have proved both democrats and republicans are under sin. Not any sin, but sin against the sanctity of life. By that line of reasoning, then most who say that they're voting their faith solely on the issue of abortion must admit to their cognitive dissonance. Furthermore that their favorite pro-life candidate also promotes murder just as much as their most hated pro-life candidate. True students of US history and policy understand that everyone has blood on their hands. No one is exempt.

So now we must question at what level we should concern sanctity of life. Is life only sacred in the womb? Is life only sacred if it's American? Is life only sacred if it lives and operates in a westernized society? Is life only sacred in political debates about the fading influence of Judeo-Christian values in America? Is life not sacred at all time? If how we vote is our seal our righteousness, nearly every voting American is in a hellish paradox.

I find it hard to believe that God can see the death of the unborn as unjust, yet somehow be ok with the murder of civilians. With the thousands of civilians to die under the hands of the Trump, Obama, and Bush administrations, it is safe to say that at least a few of them were pregnant carrying unborn children. Where then is the outrage and concern of the conservative Christian right?

Voting pro-life then doesn't really necessarily make you pro-life. So then you have no right to judge someone who views the world differently than you. We all have the right to vote our conscience.

We all have the right to vote according to the values and the principles that we believe to be most paramount.

However, we shouldn't be so quick to assume that our view of our vote is faultless. We often use the Bible to oversimplify the complexities of life to fit our human understanding. The fact of the matter is that God is sovereign over the spectrum of uncertainty. In the scripture God takes responsibility for appointing and judging both wicked and righteous rulers. He creates the both the Sauls and Davids of our day for his will.

He used Cyrus's who knew him not, and Pharaoh's whose heart was hardened against him to accomplish his will and his word. He reigns supreme and sovereign in the international order. Daniel told us plainly that "the most high rules the kingdom of men" (Daniel 4:17).

THE IDOL OF AMERICAN EXCEPTIONALISM

God cannot heal who we pretend to be. He can only heal who we admit that we are. We must confess our sins, our shorting comings, and our faults if we expect to receive God's grace. James 5:5 lets us know that "God resists the proud, But gives grace to the humble." There are many believers that are hindered in their walk with God because they're trying to present a faultless image to a Holy God that can see every crack and crevice of imperfection.

What we often think makes us righteous is a stench in his nostrils. Furthermore the prophet Isaiah says that our righteousness amounts to nothing more than "filthy rags." For that reason we can only truly obtain righteousness through our reception of Christ's work on the cross. As finite humans with blind spots we can place no stock in our own view of our moral excellence.

Our religious moralism that subtly professes that we can earn our salvation and righteousness gives us a source of pride. As the Apostle Paul eloquently argues, if we are "justified by works" then we have "something to boast about." But because we have faith in Christ, who has sanctified us, salvation comes as a "free gift." We walk in what Christ worked for meaning that we do good works to glorify our redeemer not to try to prove to our redeemer that we're worthy enough for his gift. Our good works, which don't save us of themselves, then become the fruit of God's work in Christ for us.

In other words, you're not saved because you pray and fast. Prayer and fasting are importantly biblical disciplines, but you are saved "by grace through faith." You are not saved because you go to church. Going to church is an important part of being a fully engaged and living participant in the body of Christ, but you are not saved by your church attendance. You are saved by grace through faith. Furthermore we are not saved by our choice to support what some believe to be sound biblical principles found in conservative candidates. Nor are we saved because we espouse the biblical notions of justice and human rights which some progressive candidates emphasize. We are saved by grace through faith.

The legalistic form of Christianity that has abandoned the gospel of grace toward a works based salvation has been intertwined with American evangelical political views creating a very toxic mixture.

Many believe that in order to be a born-again Christian one must profess faith in the central platform of the conservative movement. In other words, if you support Biden, you're not Christian and furthermore you're a part of the antichrist agenda.

It follows then that if you support President Trump, then you're a part of the chosen ones who really know the truth and are the real ones working for God. There are many dangers in this line of binary reasoning. The first and foremost being, that such a position does not line up with scripture.

As we discussed, political views are not a requisite for salvation and a true academic analysis of many policy measures reveals that many political issues are too complex to have a simple for or against, binary solution. Being a pro-life advocate and being justified before Christ are not equivalent.

The danger that American Christianity faces, is that the evangelical movement has meshed religious views, moralism, and political views. They've made it a "moral obligation" to think the same politically.[xi] Many leaders have equated their view of the American political landscape with the Bible.

Whenever we equate our human reasoning to be equal to the scriptures, we've landed in Pharisee territory and we're cheapening the gospel. The Pharisees merged the traditions of men with the word of God, thereby blocking them from seeing the Messiah that they were praying and seeking for.

I fear America, that today, we are just as blind as the Pharisees who had a religious form of godliness, but ultimately denied the power of God.

The Apostle Paul urged the saints of God in Rome to avoid the mistake that many of us are presently making. With a fervent heart he wrote "Why do you pass judgment on your brother? Or you, why do you despise your brother? For we will all stand before the judgment seat of God" (Romans 14:10).

The political climate in America has reached a seemingly unprecedented time where partisanship is concerned. The church has not been immune or an exemplar on how to respectfully disagree in love as described in Romans 14.

Instead we've demonstrated judgement and hatred towards those who vote differently than us. We call one's faith bogus and bicker and backbite creating irreparable divisions, allowing the devil to feast off of our instability.

5 One person esteems one day as better than another, while another esteems all days alike. Each one should be fully convinced in his own mind. 6 The one who observes the day, observes it in honor of the Lord.

The one who eats, eats in honor of the Lord, since he gives thanks to God, while the one who abstains, abstains in honor of the Lord and gives thanks to God. 7 For none of us lives to himself, and none of us dies to himself. 8 For if we live, we live to the Lord, and if we die, we die to the Lord. (Romans 14:5-8)

Paul urged the Romans to allow one another to live according to their personal convictions without judgement (obviously on those matters non-critical to salvation and sanctification).

We should indeed, learn to allow those who disagree with us to hold true to their personal convictions without judgment or being deemed demonic, antichrist, or false. Just because someone disagrees with us, does not imply that someone else is our enemy or that they are demonic.

God creates people who do things differently or value things differently. Part of being in the kingdom of God is learning to love and admire the diversity of his creation. The 21st century church is in existential danger because we've been comfortable disagreeing over our differences, but we've been complacent at leveraging our differences to advance the kingdom of God.

The problem is further compounded as these issues crossover into prophetic churches. Not only do leaders equate the importance of political views with biblical truth, they begin to prophecy from the place of their bias.

They speak out of presumption by attaching the word of the Lord to their own personal opinions. In our current spiritual and political climate many prophetic voices have already prejudged that republican leaders have been ordained heaven's support and backing. The danger in this view is that prejudging leads to prejudiced prophecies.

In 1 Samuel 16 the prophet Samuel anoints David as king, but he almost anointed the wrong person. Samuel assumed that God had chosen Eliab because of his appearance, however the passage let us know that God rejected Eliab for kingship and had chosen his brother David. Samuel was using his natural understanding and natural perception in order to discern God's will.

An approach like that is contradictory because we are finite and natural, but God is eternal and supernatural. Therefore his reasoning, viewpoint, and understanding transcends anything we can imagine. As Paul said "But God chose what is foolish in the world to shame the wise; God chose what is weak in the world to shame the strong (1 Corinthians 1:27).

As humans we are automatically biased toward our worldview. Prophetic voices must be careful to not use a dream, a vision, or perception that came from a biased place as a declaration of the word of the Lord.

Some may say however, "My political views come solidly from my biblical views, so how can my worldview be incorrect? I'm not Samuel basing my movement of natural appearance, but the spiritual truth of the word."

The Pharisees too based their world view off of the Holy Scriptures, yet vehemently rejected the King of Kings that God sent into the world. The scriptures may be holy and true, but our interpretation of them is often flawed and limited. Just because someone has a biblical worldview does not always imply that their worldview is based on the truth of God's word or in line with what the Holy Spirit is doing in the present hour. The Pharisees had the letter of the law which brought death, but neglected the spirit that breathed life.

A prophetic voice that cannot be subject to their own biases and be accurate when they speak regarding matters that they're invested in. Samuel's bias wasn't stronger than his sensitivity to the Spirit of God, so he was still able to hear God redirect him, when he was headed the wrong way. Because many of us are so filled with our own political and theological views we can't even hear God if he's shouting that we're going the wrong way.

If we use a leader's party or particular policy views that we agree with as the origin of a prophetic word, we ought not to expect to see it come to pass.

Nowhere in scripture is God bound to raise up biblical or Christian political leaders for a nation. Biblically speaking God has appointed many rulers who were disobedient to him and his way. Let's take King Saul as a simple case study. We know that God literally appointed him by the hands of Samuel.

Samuel speaking as an oracle of God forewarned the children of Israel that he would take their property, livestock, and even people and use them for his own gain. Samuel mentions that they would cry out to God because of the unrighteous nature of their political leader. In this context God had no interest in finding someone most versed or most obedient in the Torah. His objective was the humbling of a people, so he chose an imperfect leader.

We see God use whether the unrighteous or even pagan worshippers as a pattern not only when God wants to humble a nation, but when he wants to exalt one. Take King Cyrus for example: "In the first year of Cyrus king of Persia, that the word of the LORD by the mouth of Jeremiah might be fulfilled, the LORD stirred up the spirit of Cyrus king of Persia" (2 Chronicles 2:37-38).

God used Cyrus, who was not Jewish nor was he a prophet. God upholds his Word, not our political ideologies and concepts. He likely practiced an ancient Persian religion called Zoroastrianism which influenced how he drove policy in his kingdom.[xii]

But why would God be in the business of appointing leaders that don't serve him? The prophet Isaiah gives us our answer by declaring a word over the life of King Cyrus.

I am the Lord, and there is no other, besides me there is no God; I equip you, though you do not know me, 6 that people may know, from the rising of the sun and from the west, that there is none besides me; I am the Lord, and there is no other 7 I form light and create darkness; I make well-being and create calamity; I am the Lord, who does all these things. -Isaiah 45:5-7

The Lord said that we would equip Cyrus even though Cyrus did not know him. Why? Because "I am the Lord" and the Lord is sovereign. He wanted the word that he spoke long ago to be fulfilled and chose to do it through Cyrus.

God did not need a righteous Old Testament prophet or a holy priest to accomplish his will in the Earth. He accomplishes his purpose through anyone he chooses. This can be said not only of Cyrus, but Nebuchadnezzar and many other biblical figures.

God chooses who he wishes to uphold his word and he doesn't need our help or support to do that. As Daniel the prophet learned the "Most High rules the kingdom of men and gives it to whom he will and sets over it the lowliest of men" (Daniel 4:17). Whether democrat or republican, liberal or conservative, atheist or spirit filled, God is sovereign and he runs the show.

Therefore the theology that God requires Christian leaders or leaders that hold biblical values to hold office for his will to be accomplished is inaccurate. Prophetic voices who hold this faulty doctrine, will be prone to prophesying in error regarding political, national, and global events.

Note one can be accurate in the realm of personal prophecy but utterly compromised and biased in global affairs. This will explain why some prophetic voices prophesied Mitt Romney would beat President Obama and win two terms. It also explains why many seasoned prophetic voices claimed that Obama was the antichrist or how some refuse to acknowledge any of the moral shortcomings of President Trump.

Bias not only creates blind spots, but has a voice. If we're not careful we will see and perceive from our biases and claim that they're from God. We can dream, see, sense, and perceive from a bias and be led into a delusion.

Many prophetic voices have been trained to want to accomplish something that God isn't even interested in. At some level they would love to see a theocracy in America. While that may seem like a good idea to some, I hope by the end of this book you'll have some level of understanding of why that's unbiblical and dangerous.

FROM ZERO TO
SEVEN MOUNTAINS

So if God's sovereignty transcends, political parties and even whether someone believes in him, how did we arrive at a state in American politics where we believe that one party is God ordained, while the other hell ordained? The answer to that question doesn't begin in the US, but in 19th century Europe.

In 1827 an English parishioner by the name of John Darby had a horse riding accident that left him convalescent where he spent considerable time studying the Bible.[xiii] Darby came out with a new interpretation of the scripture that would end up being popular among mainstream denominations in America.

Darby's interpretation of the Bible introduced what is known as premillennialism dispensationalism. In a premillennial interpretation of the Book of Revelation, Jesus returns before his millennial reign on the Earth. Not only did Darby believe that Jesus would return before the one thousand years of peace on the Earth, Darby believed that things in the world would get progressively worse until what he described as a rapture of the church would occur. He believed true believers would be raptured or suddenly taken from the earth to make way from the Earth.

Darby believed that the Earth would get increasingly wicked with time. He believed that it was the church's duty to separate itself from the world and its wickedness and not engage in civil society. Instead of making an impact on a world that's going to get progressively worse anyway, he thought it was better for believers to simply wait for the rapture.

John Darby's rapture theology was not immediately received, especially in America. Darby's revelations came during a time of seemingly unprecedented prosperity for the young nation (mainly for white landowners). The United States was expanding into new territories and the concept of a divine extension of America's borders was prevalent so Darby's teachers were received with great skepticism.

It was also a great time for the church as there were many great revivals with thousands coming to the Lord, so the concept that the world needed to get worse before Christ's return wasn't sticking with the American church.

As time went on things in the United States did not stay so rosy. Ultimately the land went on to experience its most bloody time in history, the Civil War. Millions of people died in the war and battle fields were reminiscent of Armageddon.

Darby's bleak outlook began to gain more traction because of the dark nature of the world and seeing that they were coming to some type of and some type of great combination with such hideous destruction on the battlefield in such extreme loss of life the Americans began to more so adopt some of Darby's teachings.[xiv]

Furthermore white evangelicals were very concerned by the state of the country and the church was split over the morality of slavery. Immigration continued in the United States and Catholics who did not have that same moral views came over to the United States making evangelicals feel insecure and concerned about the progress in the history of the country and they felt that things were progressing to some evil end.[xv]

Despite what they perceived as dark cultural shifts in America, not all white evangelicals became fans of Darby and his premillennial theology. Two distinct camps formed known as the radical evangelicals who believed the church should disengage with the world and liberal evangelicals who believed otherwise.

A series of 20th century events eventually gave the radical evangelicals the upper hand in their doctrinal war. The sinking of the titanic, World War II, and the return of the Jews to Palestine made the world again seem apocalyptic. Furthermore the publication of the Scofield Reference Bible made Darby's theology mainstream.[xvi]
The climate of this time in history gave Darby's rapture theology more clout and the radical evangelicals weren't considered so radical anymore. They began to call themselves fundamentalist Christians.[xvii]

The fundamentalists were led by a minister named William B Riley. Riley was troubled by what he believed to be a modernist agenda that was taking over the American landscape. Riley, unlike his predecessor, Darby, believed that Christians should engage in politics.

Riley said "When the Church is regarded as the body of God-fearing, righteous-living men, then, it ought to be in politics, and as a powerful influence."[xviii] He believed that believers should shape government and policy. In addition to the advent of theological liberalism in mainline protestant denominations, Riley was most concerned with the teaching evolution in public schools.[xix]

Riley's pastoral network, World Christian Fundamentals Association, lobbied for anti-evolution bills in multiple states. After getting an anti-evolution bill passed in Tennessee, the new law was challenged in court, leading to what's known as the Scopes Monkey Trial. The case garnered national attention, putting the very strict fundamentalist beliefs of Riley and his colleagues on public display. Although the fundamentalists won the trial, they made some very embarrassing missteps bringing national humiliation. The general public did not regard many of their extreme viewpoints.

From this point, the fundamentalists began to disengage from politics and move toward a more Darby-esque approach to engaging in the world- that is disengaging from it. Fundamentalists remained in the shadows, occupying no particular political party until a man by the name of Paul Weyrich came on the scene.

He had been looking for a way to mobilize evangelicals as a significant voting block by leveraging moral issues, but hadn't found much success. For two decades, he tried "pornography, prayer in schools, the proposed Equal Rights Amendment to the Constitution, even abortion" but none of these issues seemed to motivate them politically.[xx]

In the 1960s many evangelical leaders did not consider abortion to be sinful. In fact Linda Coffee, who filed the original Roe v. Wade suit in favor of abortion rights, was a southern Baptist. She not only went to church camp, but "her grandfather was a deacon...she went to Sunday school, played softball, and sang in a choir."[xxi]

The Baptist press in response to the Roe v. Wade decision said that "The Roman Catholic hierarchy insists that the Supreme Court blundered by making an immoral, anti-religious and unjustified decision. It has vowed to continue the fight against relaxed abortion laws.

However, most other religious bodies and leaders, who have expressed themselves, approve the decision. Social, welfare and civil rights workers hailed the decision with enthusiasm."[xxii] In other words the anti-abortion stance was seen largely as catholic not evangelical. Many evangelical leaders in fact were more concerned about the government's ability to interfere with the decision between a woman and her doctor than morality.

With several moral and societal issues incapable of galvanizing the fundamentalist base, Paul Weyrich turned to another pain point, racial segregation. At this time, many fundamentalists used their pulpits to justify segregation. Take Baptist minister Henry Lyons Jr as an example. In one sermon he emphatically claimed "...there is not one passage in your Bible or mine that teaches racial integration-not one...anyone who works against the work of God in the separation of the races, is violating the law of God."[xxiii]

After the IRS removed tax exempt status from segregated Christian schools, many evangelical fundamentalists' leaders were outraged. The revocation of Bob Jones University's tax exempt status "alerted the Christian school community about what could happen with government interference."[xxiv] Paul Weyrich saw their frustration as an opportunity. Joined by Jerry Falwell, Weyrich mobilized evangelical leaders around segregation and state's rights.

This message however would not be palatable among mass evangelical flock, so Weyrich had to find another issue to motivate the flock at-large. By the late seventies, the issue of abortion began to broaden beyond the catholic base. The "small but undeniably fervent group"[xxv] of anti-abortionists led to senate race upsets. Weyrich saw that he would be able to use abortion as a fuel to mobilize evangelicals into a new voting block for the Republican Party. Today evangelicals, a group that was largely apolitical at one point, is now the backbone of the pro-life movement and one of the pillars of the Republican Party.

Historically speaking, several of the defining moments of the evangelical movement are centered on Darby's premillennial rapture theology, racism, and abortion. These issues thereby are the lens by which many white evangelicals in particular approached, understood, studied, and taught the scripture in the 20th century. These biases have not only crept into interpreting the bible, but the declaration of prophecy.

In review of prophetic words spoken by even some greats of faith the 20th century, I've found that some even declared words based on the McCarthyism hysteria of the 50s. We must be careful not to fall to the biases of our culture and understanding. If they can error then, we can error now. If we have poor theology, and even a poor and biased understanding of history we can be carried away by our biases and not by the Holy Spirit.

Darby's premillennialist teaching has led to a lens of scripture where we see every major negative event global event as a sign of the coming of the Lord. Hyper-futurist teaching has led many to presumptuously declare the return of the Lord on specific dates.

Many extreme teaching and prophecy comes from the fact that many of us inherited our end-times views not directly from Darby's writings nor the Bible, but Left Behind movies. Even some bible teachers have done little diligence beyond inherited teaching and movie watching.

Because of this teaching people have believed that everything from social security numbers to barcodes to the COVID-19 vaccine are the mark of the beast.

Many people prophesy not from a place of clarity or sound judgement, but faulty theology and hysteria. Through teaching and prophecy many leaders have created a fear based and anxiety driven gospel that has led many to leave the faith. A perusal of the #RaptureAnxiety hashtag from 2017 is filled with horror stories of many who left the faith as they were trained to be more moved by the fear of being left behind than by faith in Christ.

We have given our affections not to Christ above, but to secondary matters while neglecting the fundamentals of the faith and leaving a trail of lost souls behind. The fundamentals of the faith are being repressed not by a liberal anti-Christ agenda, but because the representatives for Christ have given ancillary matters the weight and focus that Christ and his gospel should have had all along.

Today few teach the extremes of Darby's call to be separate from society. Instead many instead are pursuing the seven mountains of influence. My concern is many believers seek to advance in the from the seat of Christian narcissism.

Modern prosperity gospel theology has led many of us to believe that the earth belongs to Christians more than it does to unbelievers. Furthermore many of us believe more in our ability to decree and declare than God's sovereignty. I'm concerned that some now are using prophecy to invent a theology where we try to take dominion over things that ultimately belong to God and not to man.

As believers participate in civil society we must understand that God did not call us to become Christian nationalists. Christ did not try to Christianize Rome. The apostles did see making governments Christian as their objective. Instead they prioritized the gospel and made disciples. On whatever mountain a believer stands, one must acknowledge that God owns that mountain. Even if atheists dominate it, he still sovereignly reigns over it.

I'm not arguing there's anything wrong with believers looking to influence the world and arise, but let us be sure to be led by the Holy Spirit and not the voice of ambition. A voice that whispers and justifies moral missteps and failings for the sake of progress. A voice that makes us entitled to take dominion rather than submissive to God's sovereignty. If not, once again many will find themselves on the wrong side of history.

THE NEW GOLDEN CALF

The American church as diverse in thought and opinion as she is has typically held the view that the moral fitness of a president is a requisite for office. Standing as a moral conscience for the nation, the church has been known to speak up regarding the ethics of presidential candidates and even office holders. For instance, Pastor and theologian John McArthur not only deemed that President Clinton was no longer fit to serve in office because of his adultery and lying, but went as far as to denounce Clinton's salvation.

"The president said some weeks ago that nobody should be concerned about his sexual sin. It was an issue, he said, between himself, his family, he said, and our God. Let me tell you something about his god. His god is not the God of the Bible. The God of the Bible is not pro feminism, pro homosexual, pro lesbian, and pro fornication, pro adultery. That's not the God of the Bible. He's not pro deception, He's not pro lying. You see, he has the same god that all who reject the true God have and you can meet him every morning; he's there in your mirror."[xxvi]

McArthur's views of President Clinton stands in stark contrast to his comments regarding President Trump. In an interview on politics, conservative pundit Ben Shapiro asks McArthur in an interview "As religious people, how should we approach...candidates who may not be personally moral, but forward our priorities? McArthur's response was very telling. He says, "The presidency is not a moral job. It's not a position of moral authority it never has been. We don't want to make it into that."[xxvii]

On one hand McArthur finds that Bill Clinton is unfit for office due to moral failings, yet in a discussion during the presidency of one who is willing to "forward" his priorities, the morality of the office holder is irrelevant. This bias is at the heart of the toxic marriage between politics and the evangelical church. A bias that has stirred erroneous prophecy, shipwrecking the faith of many.

For the sake of our priorities, we have been willing to turn a blind eye to the depravity of our favorite political leaders. We can infer McArthur's priorities from his statement regarding Clinton. He, like many evangelicals, wants to see America look like the Bible and the Bible look like America. The only problem is, there's no bible for that. Paul did not seek to make Rome look like the Bible and the bible like Rome. Contrary to popular belief America is a secular nation and we have no scripture that says the nation's founders had a covenant with God.

The American church has such a lust for a theocracy that many in Americans pulpits are willing to obtain it at any costs. Even the cost of the witness of the American church. Many equated standing up for righteousness with standing up for Trump and conservative ideologies.

The angel of light has slowly architected a mass assault on our witness by training us into believing that by our political stance is evangelistic in nature. We have come to a place in American church history that when we say Jesus, people think Donald Trump. By placing our hopes, ambitions, and aspirations in a fallible man of greatly questionable moral stature.

By casting our crowns to serve Trump rather than Jesus, that moral facade that the American church had been hiding behind for years was ripped away. As President Trump's moral failings increased so did our defense of him regardless of how derelict and disparaging they were. The nation noticed and the exodus of young Christians was exasperated.

Souls of all backgrounds have left and are leaving not only churches, but faith in Christ because of our contradictory witness. We are in a crisis because we sold the deliverance and salvation of many for our "priorities."

But again how did we get here? Was it only because of Darby, segregation, and abortion? The political climate in America has always had some level of division, but this level of polarization is unique. According to Pew research "Republicans and Democrats are more divided along ideological lines – and partisan antipathy is deeper and more extensive – than at any point in the last two decades." [xxviii]

This division that affects the church, but extends beyond the church did not begin with the church. Much of it actually didn't even begin in America. Much of the polarization that we're seeing today actually came from Russia. In the aftermath of the 2016 election, the Republican led Senate Intelligence Committee investigated Russian interference in the US election. The results are startling and have implications on the church and even the prophetic movement.

According the committee's report, led by republican Senator Marco Rubio, Russian operatives masquerading as Americans "used targeted advertisements, intentionally falsified news articles, self-generated content, and social media platform tools to interact with and attempt to deceive tens of millions of social media users in the United States." [xxix]
Russian spies were responsible for deploying the real fake news. Not the ad hominem attacks President Trump hurled at journalists and traditional media organizations, but actual propaganda created by the Kremlin to influence American thought.

According to the report, Russia's aim was "polarize Americans on the basis of societal, ideological, and racial differences, provoked real world events, and was part of a foreign government's covert support of Russia's favored candidate in the U.S. presidential election"[xxx]

Although the Kremlin targeted all facets of American ideology on both the left and the right ranging from Black Lives Matter to the Proud Boys, I focus here on their interference with Christian thought.

They spent major ad dollars building social media platforms to spread divisive propaganda and increase polarization in the United States, one page Russian operatives made was a seemingly faith based account called "Army of Jesus" with over 200,000 followers on Facebook. The page would post Christian content to attract believers. A key in propaganda is gaining trust and telling enough of the truth so that your propaganda is received.

The Kremlin's objective was to spread not only misinformation about Hilary Clinton, but emotional and divisive misinformation. They used Army of Jesus among other pages to do so. The report lists a series of messages from the page:

October 26, 2016: "There has never been a day when people did not need to walk with Jesus."
October 29, 2016: "I've got Jesus in my soul. It's the only way I know …. Watching every move I make, guiding every step I take!"
October 31, 2016: "Rise and shine-realize His blessing!" .,
October 31, 2016: "Jesus will always be by your side. Just reach out to Him and you'll see!" ~
November 1, 2016: "HILLARY APPROVES REMOVAL OF GOD FROM THE PLEDGE OF ALLEGIANCE."
 November 2, 2016: "Never hold on anything [sic] tighter than you holding unto God!"

Note that the faith based posts are surrounded by misinformation about Hilary Clinton. Of course posts like these would be accompanied by fake news articles depicting Hillary a god hating, bible hating person.

Conspiracy theory websites, fake news articles, and social media accounts from Russia spies all had their hand in shaping public opinion in America (again, the political left was not exempt from this propaganda).

Now as we described in Unmasking Prophetic Bias Book 1: Covid-19, End Times Hysteria, and the Christian Church, the more you're exposed to false information and conspiracies, the more prone you are to believe them regardless of the facts. This is known scientifically as the illusory truth effect. The more we scroll and digest content meant to make us biased the more we will believe it and the more biased we will become.

Christians and their leaders were prime consumers of polarizing Russian misinformation that allowed many believers to see the 2020 election a literal good vs evil showdown. This was a part of Moscow's objective. Putin's information war helped us to create idols out of lies.

An idol is anything we put before Christ. For many President Trump and the Republican Party became an idol. When we have an idol, the spirit that empowers the idol we serve is responsible for sustaining us.

Any attempt to challenge our devotion or submission to the idol is met with a demonic resistance. When we're devoted to an idol there's an irrational need to protect and defend our relationship with it regardless of what the facts are.

We saw the golden-calf of Trump rise when bible teachers could not challenge or question prophecies regarding President Trump's second term. The strongman keeping people in bondage had believers picking Facebook fights and calling one another demons in ways I'd never imagine.

After Prophet Jeremiah Johnson publicly apologized for incorrectly prophesying Trump's second term, he received "death threats and thousands upon thousands of emails from Christians saying the nastiest and most vulgar things."[xxxi] This extreme nature of the response from Christians shows that many of us gave more of our intimacy to our idea of Trump and Christian nationalism than to Christ.

Many believers have spent more time on YouTube watching conspiracy theory websites like Info Wars, Breitbart, and Epoch Times than in prayer or Bible reading. As I explained in Unmasking Prophetic Bias Book 1, websites like these are drenched with the spirit of error. They source their information from conspiracy theory internet forums and even foreign operatives to play to the biases of the American populous.

While credible journalism relies on interviews, primary source documents, and government contacts to investigate stories, top conspiracy theory content creators like Alex Jones admittedly rely on internet forums to source information and create stories. \

Oxford defines gossip as "casual or unconstrained conversation or reports about other people, typically involving details that are not confirmed as being true." "Information" from random people on internet forums about politicians, governments, and leaders is no more than global gossip.

"The words of a whisperer are like delicious morsels; they go down into

the inner parts of the body." - Proverbs 18:8

Gossip is tasteful and seductive, but dark and carnal reaching the inner being. As many people consumed digital end-times gossip, which lacked rigorous political analysis or investigative journalism, the lies began to reach deep inside them mutating their soul and corrupting their inner man to believe lies rather than the truth.

Prophets and prophetic people filled themselves with conspiracy after conspiracy regardless of what reality said. With over 60 election lawsuit losses (even from conservative Trump appointee judges) and a finalized electoral college, many prophets continue to hold onto their illusion that Trump will win. Furthermore their angry fans stand in misplaced faith with them believing a delusion.

It's no surprise that even after all of this, many are prophesying the same thing. Many prophetic voices in America have been speaking from the voice of their idols from the beginning, we just didn't realize it. When Trump said Covid-19 was a conspiracy so did the prophets.

When Trump said there was mass election fraud so did the prophets. Like the four hundred prophets that stood in Ahab's court, many premier prophetic voices have come under the delusion of a lying spirit because of their self-indoctrination with conspiracy theories.

Ahab's prophets led him into an unwinnable battle that caused his demise. Several of today's prophetic voices have helped lead many in this nation into a battle that can kill their faith.

They prophesied the righteousness of Trump while ignoring his moral failings and played a significant part in the attempted coup d'état on Capitol Hill. Some prophets and evangelical leaders in prior Trump rallies had even been calling for physical violence if necessary.

Mixed with narcissistic dominionaire theology where because we're God's children we have a right to change anything in the world we don't prefer, people went to the capital not only to protest, but to take over. Prophets took pictures and streamed their prayer groups live from the capital all while justifying the gross darkness descend upon Capitol Hill.

No longer did the prophets that proclaimed Blue Lives Matter, declare judgement on those who harmed police officers during those events. Apparently God was silent on the matter. The brazen, erratic, and bullish nature that we saw on President Trump's Twitter feed manifested upon our nation's capital.

The spirit that was upon the White House was the spirit that was upon many of our premier and trusted prophetic voices. The prophetic movement in the American church is obviously not the sole source of what we witnessed, but we do have a part to play.

You may say, "I never prophesied anything like that. I have nothing to do with it." That may be true, but prayer and repentance is often far too individualistic. Daniel, a holy man of God, when praying for his nation did not merely say "forgive them," but rather "we have sinned and done wrong and acted wickedly and rebelled, turning aside from your commandments and rules" (Daniel 9:5).

Isaiah, another righteous servant of God, recognized not only his humanity but that of those around him when he cried " Woe is me! for I am undone; because I am a man of unclean lips, and I dwell in the midst of a people of unclean lips" (Isaiah 6:5). We must always understand our fallibility. We must be beacons for restoration and hope for those who seek to recover.

Their failure is our failure. Their embarrassment is our embarrassment. There's no hiding it. But furthermore their success is our success. We are one body serving one God.

The prophetic movement, moreover the church at large can move past this only when we come to understand that at any given time we can all be carried away. We can be carried away by our biases, our fears, our theology to the point where we can no longer see Jesus Christ.

We can be carried away to the point where we believe a lie rather than the truth and we miss the moment we were created for by misrepresenting God. I penned these words, not because I believe I'm the authority or the expert on this subject matter, but rather because I recognize that I can be the subject of the next person's scribal correction if I find myself away from the place of grace. Let's take refuge in our God not in our opinions before we all get swept away.

WERE THE TRUMP PROPHECIES CONDITIONAL?

Many prophetic voices declared emphatically without reservation or condition that President Donald Trump would be elected for a second term. Let's take a moment and look at just a few popular prophecies from noted charismatic leaders. Take for instance one of the pastors of a Las Vegas church who prophesied publicly and directly to Trump during a church service.

"Good morning Mr. President Trump. It's good to see you there. At 4:30 the Lord said to me "I'm going to give your president a second wind. Now this has three meanings. A win. You will be the president again. A win that when an athlete is running a marathon there's such a thing as a second wind where...He has made your lungs, your body, your strength. He has made it in such high pressured places in the last four years and even before that and the Lord said that he is ready for the next four years. And I'm giving him a second win. Understand that? And there's also this. If you add 'd' it's the Holy Spirit. And the Lord showed me today; He showed me today that you were coming to get a second wind of that second another in filling of the Holy Spirit. Because the Holy Spirit makes you able to finish take this to the end Mr. President. And then he said to me that you were the apple of his eye. And that's what we are friends and that he's protecting you like he is protecting the ancient foundations of our nation. God wants to be in

the middle of our nation and that I believe this is it right here."[xxxii]

Another evangelical leader spoke with great boldness concerning Trump's certain election fate.

"Without question, Trump is going to win the election...that's a given. After he's sworn in, then trouble is going to happen. He's going to be challenged by the Chinese as you couldn't believe. We'll be faced probably with some kind of a war. The North Koreans are going to have nuclear weapons. They're going to threaten us...After Trump is sworn in, we're going to see civil disobedience in America that will just be mind boggling. There will be at least two attempts on the President's life...The fulfillment will take place of Ezekiel 38's prophecy.[xxxiii]

In an interview, another charismatic preacher made some very interesting proclamations regarding not only the length of Trump's tenure, but that of his successors.

"He caught me up to heaven, literally, months and months and months before and He said, 'I've chosen Trump and people won't like it and they won't understand it but that doesn't matter right now because I'm going to change America and I need him. He's an all-American boy that is all for America, and he is smart, he can't be bought, he can't be moved, and he cannot be controlled.' And He said, 'He will know me and he will hear my voice.' You better step back, because this is God's time. In the next election they won't win either...We're going to have Trump for 8 years, Pence for 8 years and then the one Pence picks. I'm just throwing this out there because the Father is saying this. For 24 years we're going to have God in the White House."[xxxiv]

Even after the presidential election was called, many famed prophetic voices doubled down on what they said prior. One notable speaker recorded a video from the nation's capital on the day of the infamous January 6th capitol riot that "The Lord has anointed and appointed Trump to be president for a second term. It's not 2024. It's right now in the next couple of weeks."[xxxv]

Another prophet said that ""Either a lying spirit has filled the mouths of numerous trusted prophetic voices in America or Donald J. Trump really has won the presidency and we are witnessing a diabolical and evil plan unfold to steal the election."[xxxvi] He of course believed the former, but has since come out confessing and repenting that he gave an erroneous prophecy concerning Trump's second term.

When you go through the multitude of election prophecies touted by leaders from all across the evangelical spectrum, the above transcripts are typical examples of the characteristics that many of them share.

They are very de facto and bold prophecies that are insistent that Trump will occupy the White House as POTUS for a second term directly after his 2016 term. They emphasize that God has been handpicked and chosen for this role. They imply that God himself backs Trump and that there's no alternative future. There are no conditions presented and they are declared as if we should expect to see the manifestation of these prophetic words.

I have not been able to find one biblical example where a leadership change was predicted in scripture and God silently revoked the previous utterance. I don't think we would have heard of the Old Testament prophet Samuel if he anointed Saul to be king and the word did not come to pass.

I don't think Samuel would have been able to retain his reputation if he prophesied that David would be king and the word doesn't come to pass because Saul killed him and there was no forewarning.

Predictive prophecies without condition in the bible came to pass. Although David endured a decade's long war before taking the throne, he still overcame and the word came to pass. In other words, God is strong enough to ensure his word will come to pass because he declares it with opposition in mind. The scriptural precedent for God redirecting a word because of someone's actions is that God announces the change ahead of time.

For instance, God revoked a promise from the lineage of Eli the priest because of his negligence and disobedience.

Therefore the Lord, the God of Israel, declares: 'I promised that your house and the house of your father should go in and out before me forever,' but now the Lord declares: 'Far be it from me, for those who honor me I will honor, and those who despise me shall be lightly esteemed. 31 Behold, the days are coming when I will cut off your strength and the strength of your father's house, so that there will not be an old man in your house. (1 Samuel 2:30-31).

In this instance God did not simply allow Eli and all of his lineage to die out before releasing the word of judgement. He notified him ahead of time. The purpose of predictive prophecy is to explain things ahead of time, not to explain events after they occur.

Another clear example is in the life of the prophet Isaiah. He initially prophecies that King Hezekiah would die soon. Hezekiah prays and then God gives the prophet another word.

Then the word of the Lord came to Isaiah: 5 "Go and say to Hezekiah, Thus says the Lord, the God of David your father: I have heard your prayer; I have seen your tears. Behold, I will add fifteen years to your life. 6 I will deliver you and this city out of the hand of the king of Assyria, and will defend this city. 7 "This shall be the sign to you from the Lord, that the Lord will do this thing that he has promised: 8 Behold, I will make the shadow cast by the declining sun on the dial of Ahaz turn back ten steps." So the sun turned back on the dial the ten steps by which it had declined. (Isaiah 38:4-7)

God didn't silently give Hezekiah 15 more years and then tell him in his last year that he ended up changing his mind. He told Hezekiah about the extension of his life soon after his prayer. Furthermore he even gave the king a sign confirming what was to come concerning his life and victory in battle.

Some proponents of the Trump prophecies cite Jonah's prophecy to Nineveh as an example that fits the present scenario. Jonah prophesied "Yet forty days, and Nineveh shall be overthrown" (Jonah 3:5).

The people fasted and repented and the scripture tells us that "When God saw what they did, how they turned from their evil way, God relented of the disaster that he had said he would do to them, and he did not do it." While it is true that Jonah made a de facto statement concerning the fate of Nineveh, again we see that God spoke regarding the fact that he decided to spare the land.

The book of Jonah does not end with at fifth verse of the third chapter. Instead it continues onto a conversation accounting as to why God decided to spare the people. This example cannot be applied in defense of Trump prophecies because they released no other words detailing that God was going in a different direction.

Furthermore Jonah's prophecy is not merely a predictive prophecy, like the emergence of a world leader. Jonah's word to Nineveh is a warning. There are several passages that let us know that warnings from God are often conditional by default. He warns us to give space for repentance.

For instance Joel notes the mercy of God that comes with repentance "Return to the Lord your God, for he is gracious and merciful, slow to anger, and abounding in steadfast love and he relents over disaster. Who knows whether he will not turn and relent, and leave a blessing behind him, a grain offering and a drink offering for the Lord your God? (Joel 2:13-14). Popular Trump prophecies were not spoken as predictive warnings, but rather as predictive certainties and should be judged as such.

If God initially declared that Trump would be a two term president (I do not believe that he did), but revoked that promise from his life, the same charismatic leaders that publicly proclaimed that God anointed him, should have also publicly declared that the change and the reason behind it before the election.

Many prophetic leaders prophesied and declared judgements and curses over America after Trump's defeat, however their words hold no weight because they spoke after the fact. Anyone can "hear" God's redirection after a word doesn't come to pass. There's no legitimate way to judge words from what I call "after prophets" which are those who like to say "I knew or I had a word or I felt such and so" after the fact.

For instance one prophetic leader said that he had a feeling on the night of the election that God had changed his mind. Conveniently he shared this a few days after the certification of the Electoral College rather than on the night he had the supposed impression from the Lord. Anyone can get a feeling in the pit of their stomach during election night where results are not looking in favor of what we prophesied earlier.

In summary I do not see a biblical precedent for God announcing a political leader and only releasing the conditions of their receipt of the office until after they are unable to occupy the office.

Many however are saying "Wait! What about the late Kim Clement's prophecy about Trump and his second term." You may be shocked to know that popular prophecies circulating YouTube from Kim Clement do not say that Trump will have a second term.

Those prophecies online are different prophecies that Kim Clement released over several years that people spliced together in a way that sounds like Prophet Clement prophecies a two term presidency for Donald Trump.

Clement's ministry has a YouTube page called "Kim Clement Prophecy | The Trump Prophecies, ISIS, Socialism, Russia, China." The video which was uploaded in 2018 contains in their words "a collection of prophecies from Kim Clement regarding things that have happened and things that are yet to happen. These prophecies range in date from 2007 to 2014."

According the video on April 4, 2007, Kim Clement prophesied "Trump shall become a Trumpet. You didn't hear me. Trump shall become a Trumpet. Are you listening to me? I will raise up Trump to become a Trumpet and Bill Gates to open up the Gate for the financial realm for the church, says the spirit of the living God."[xxxvii]

In a separate utterance three years later in Arizona, Clement said:

"There will be a praying president, not a religious one. For I will fool the people, says the Lord. I will fool the people, yes I will. The one that is chosen shall go in and they shall say, "He has hot blood." For the spirit of God says he will bring the walls of protection on this country in a greater way. And the economy of this country shall change rapidly, says the Lord of hosts. Listen to the word of the Lord. I will put at your helm for two terms, a president that will pray, but he will not be a praying president when he starts. I will put him in office and then I will baptize him with the Holy Spirit and my power says the Lord of Hosts."

Several videos on YouTube stich these and other Clement prophecies together, however Clement does not mention Trump or any other names regarding his two term prophecy or the impeachment prophecy.

I won't speak to the accuracy of these prophecies however, I will address the nature of prophecy. If we assume that these prophecies are true then we can't assume that they all refer to one person. Presidential elections are every four years and popular governmental prophecies from Clement come from varying time frames. He says that there is a praying president who will get two terms but does not mention a name. Applying that prophecy to President Trump is merely assumption not a promise to put faith in.

Furthermore, if we go under the assumption these prophecies are accurate and that Prophet Clement is speaking of the same person, Trump would not fit because he also prophesied the following:

They will shout "impeach, impeach" they say, but nay...They will shout "impeach, impeach" but this will not happen.[xxxviii]

President Trump is first president in history to be impeached twice. Although he was not removed from office, like Clinton he was impeached by the House of Representatives.

Furthermore some of Clement's prophecies make reference to the nature and character of the president he speaks of. For example he says that this man will be a "Man of prayer. A man of choice words. They will even say this man is not speaking enough."[xxxix] This description has no resemblance to President Trump. Even his most ardent supporters admittedly like how bold his speech is.

One YouTube commenter wrote on a video purporting that Clement's prophecies refer to Trump "My faith is solid in God in Good and in Donald Trump, for my will our will will be done on earth as it is in heaven."[xl] I believe herein rests our problem. Many have placed their faith in a man and an idea and not totally in God. For this reason many are and will be shipwrecked in faith.

BACK TO THE FOUNDATION

So where do we go from here? Back to the foundation that Christ built. We live in a time where more Christians are concerned about the lack of biblical education and prayer in public schools than they are about the stench of biblical illiteracy in their own churches.

Few churches today preach a sound and coherent gospel, yet expect secular institutions to do what many churches have been failing to do for several decades. There seems to be a great rally cry for preserving American's so-called conservative values, yet there seems to be limited conviction for sin, compassion for the lost, or desperation for God in our cultural Christianity.

Political rallies and prayer-less prayer breakfasts have become more common than earth shattering intersession or true revival. The church is very busy doing everything but what she has been called to do. Jesus gave very clear instructions in the great commission in Matthew 28:19. He instructed us to make disciples, baptize, and teach.

I believe the church has been very efficient at making disciples, just not the kind that Jesus wants. The emphasis on religious moralism by the American church has created a culture where we create disciples that have a greater resemblance to the nearest Republican politician than to Jesus Christ.

In an attempt to Christianize American culture, the church in America has garnered a reputation for contempt. The world knows what Christians hate, but not who Jesus loves. This is in part because the American branded cultural Christianity that so many love and adore has been bent on protesting what we don't want to see while not communicating God's vision for what he wants to see.

Furthermore, the evangelical movement has been guilty of trying to legislate biblical righteousness in America while neglecting that fact "the letter killeth, but the Spirit giveth life" (2 Cor. 3:6). The problem is that legislation can change laws, but it can't change hearts. God showed us this with the children of Israel and how the law was "weak through the flesh" (Rom. 8:3). Creating a modern American theocracy may change visible behavior, but it will never convert the heart or soul.

At best it can create a new generation of Pharisees who feel justified in their own morality apart from the work of the Holy Spirit. We cannot expect those who have not received the spirit of Christ to live like regenerated persons by the pen of a legislator. Christians may feel more culturally comfortable in a more "conservative" nation, but would God not be able to see beyond the superficial facade the religiosity of America (much like he does now) and still see hearts that still refuse to be sanctified by him.

In other words you can take away any "sinful liberal" policy that you wish or enforce any "righteous conservative" agenda that you desire, but the state of the nation will still be the same. Legalism isn't the way to righteousness in God's eyes. Jesus is. Therefore the church must focus on the agenda that she was called to- preaching the gospel and making disciples.

REFERENCES

[i] *Trump Trigger Pulled - PSA 101620*. (2020, October 16). [Video]. YouTube. https://www.youtube.com/watch?v=p-OAjrYIO9A

[ii] La Comisión para el Esclarecimiento Histórico (CEH). (1994). *GUATEMALA MEMORY OF SILENCE: Report of the Commission for Historical Clarificatioll Conclusions and Recommendations*. https://www.ca1.uscourts.gov/sites/ca1/files/citations/Guatemala%20Memory%20of%20Silence%20Report%20of%20the%20Commission%20for%20Historical%20Clarification%20Conclusions%20and%20Recommendations.pdf

[iii] Gamble, J. K. (1990). *INTERNATIONAL LAW IN THE REAGAN YEARS: HOW MUCH OF AN OUTLIER?* Akron Law Review. https://www.uakron.edu/dotAsset/c324b0a3-9ba9-4ef7-a05c-768d97e375a3.pdf

[iv] *Remarks by the President at the National Defense University*. (2013, May 24). Whitehouse.Gov. https://obamawhitehouse.archives.gov/the-press-office/2013/05/23/remarks-president-national-defense-university

[v] Briggs, B. (2013, July 3). *Study: US drone strikes more likely to kill civilians than US jet fire*. NBC News. https://www.nbcnews.com/news/investigations/study-us-drone-strikes-more-likely-kill-civilians-us-jet-nvna19254842

[vi] Alexander, S. (2017). *Double-Tap Warfare: Should President*

Obama Be Investigated for War Crimes? (No. 69). Florida Law Review. https://scholarship.law.ufl.edu/flr/vol69/iss1/7/

[vii] Borger, J. (2018, January 23). *US air wars under Trump: increasingly indiscriminate, increasingly opaque.* The Guardian. https://www.theguardian.com/us-news/2018/jan/23/us-air-wars-trump

[viii] Dilanian, K., & Kube, C. (2019, March 7). *Trump cancels Obama policy of reporting drone strike deaths.* NBC News. https://www.nbcnews.com/politics/donald-trump/trump-cancels-obama-policy-reporting-drone-strike-deaths-n980156

[ix] Elbagir, N. S. A. (2018, August 18). *Bomb in Yemen school bus strike was US-supplied.* CNN. https://edition.cnn.com/2018/08/17/middleeast/us-saudi-yemen-bus-strike-intl/index.html

[x] Almosawa, S., & Hubbard, B. (2018, August 9). *Saudi Coalition Airstrike Hits School Bus in Yemen, Killing Dozens.* The New York Times. https://www.nytimes.com/2018/08/09/world/middleeast/yemen-airstrike-school-bus-children.html

[xi] Cohn, A. (2019, October 9). *Ralph Reed: Evangelicals have "moral obligation" to support Trump.* The Hill. https://thehill.com/blogs/blog-briefing-room/news/464975-ralph-reed-evangelicals-have-moral-obligation-to-support-trump

[xii] History.com Editors. (2019, October 8). *Zoroastrianism.* HISTORY. https://www.history.com/topics/religion/zoroastrianism#:%7E:text=It%20was%20the%20state%20religion,to%20practice%20their%20own%20religions.

[xiii] *Letters of J. N. Darby, 3:226.* (185-). STEM Publishing. https://www.stempublishing.com/authors/darby/letters/53226E.html

[xiv] Marsh, C. (2019). *The Rapture: Cosmic Segregation or Antidote for Oppression? A Critical Response to the "Racial Ideology of Rapture" by Nathaniel P. Grimes.* The Council on Dispensational Hermeneutics. https://www.socalsem.edu/wp-content/uploads/2019/09/Cory-Marsh-CDH.pdf

[xv] NPR. (2019, June 11). *Throughline: Apocalypse Now.* NPR.Org. https://choice.npr.org/index.html?origin=https://www.npr.org/2019/06/11/731664197/apocalypse-now

[xvi] Mangum, T., & Sweetnam, M. (2009). *The Scofield Bible: Its History and Impact on the Evangelical Church.* Paternoster.

[xvii] Taylor, J. (2016, June 14). *The 4 Phases of Protestant Fundamentalism in America.* The Gospel Coalition. https://www.thegospelcoalition.org/blogs/evangelical-history/the-four-phases-of-protestant-fundamentalism-in-america/

[xviii] Larson, E. J. (1997). *Summer for the Gods: The Scopes Trial and America's Continuing Debate Over Science and Religion* (Revised ed.). Basic Books.

[xix] Linder, D. (n.d.). *Putting Evolution on the Defensive: John Nelson Darby, Dwight L. Moody, William B. Riley and the Rise of Fundamentalism in America.* Https://Famous-Trials.Com/. https://famous-trials.com/scopesmonkey/2182-fundamentalism

[xx] Balmer, R. (2014, May 27). *The Real Origins of the Religious Right.* POLITICO Magazine. https://www.politico.com/magazine/story/2014/05/religious-right-real-origins-107133

[xxi] https://www.vanityfair.com/news/2017/01/roe-v-wades-secret-heroine-tells-her-story

[xxii] Garrett, W. B. (1973). *High Court Holds Abortion To Be "A right of Privacy."* Southern Baptist Historical Library and Archives. http://media.sbhla.org.s3.amazonaws.com/3521,31-Jan-1973.pdf

[xxiii] Montgomery County Citizens' Council (Ala.). (1961). *Transcript of a public meeting held by the Montgomery County Citizens' Council at Garrett Coliseum. Foreword and transcript of Montgomery County Citizens' Council meeting, pages 1 through 24.* Alabama Department of History and Archives. https://digital.archives.alabama.gov/digital/collection/voices/id/3223

[xxiv] Balmer, R. (2014, May 27). *The Real Origins of the Religious Right.* POLITICO Magazine. https://www.politico.com/magazine/story/2014/05/religious-right-real-origins-107133

[xxv] Kneeland, D. (1978, November 13). Clark Defeat in Iowa Laid to Abortion Issue. *The New York Times.* https://www.nytimes.com/1978/11/13/archives/clark-defeat-in-iowa-laid-to-abortion-issue-national-help.html

[xxvi] McArthur, J. (1998, September 20). *The Destructive Sin of Lying, Part 1.* Grace to You. https://www.gty.org/library/sermons-library/90-196/the-destructive-sin-of-lying-part-1?fbclid=IwAR35UrmEkToWTKkclgXsLOIDF5iFthHwfegcP5cn4Q8qGRQCnuXKflHz8Eo

[xxvii] The Daily Wire. (2018, December 2). *John MacArthur | The Ben Shapiro Show Sunday Special Ep. 29* [Video]. YouTube. https://www.youtube.com/watch?v=F-ofKxfYqGw

[xxviii] *Political Polarization in the American Public.* (2019, De-

cember 31). Pew Research Center - U.S. Politics & Policy. https://www.pewresearch.org/politics/2014/06/12/political-polarization-in-the-american-public/

[xxix] SELECT COMMITTEE ON INTELLIGENCE UNITED STATES SENATE. (2019).)REPOR T OF THE REPORT 116-XX SELECT COMMITTEE ON INTELLIGENCE UNITED STATES SENATE ON RUSSIAN ACTIVE MEASURE;S CAMPAIGNS AND INTERFERENCE IN THE 2016 U.S. ELECTION ' VOLUME 2: RUSSIA'S USE OF SOCIAL MEDIA WITH ADDITIONAL VIEWS (Volume 2). https://www.intelligence.senate.gov/sites/default/files/documents/Report_Volume2.pdf

[xxx] Ibid.

[xxxi] Calagui, J. M. (2021, January 13). Prophet Jeremiah Johnson Receives Death Threats After Apologizing For "Wrong" Prophecy About President Trump. Christianity Daily. http://www.christianitydaily.com/articles/10507/20210113/prophet-jeremiah-johnson-receives-death-threats-after-apologizing-for-wrong-prophecy-about-president-trump.htm

[xxxii] "The Lord said to me, 'I am going to give your president a second win.' ". (2020, October 18). [Video]. YouTube. https://www.youtube.com/watch?v=baa7qLudRus

[xxxiii] Pat Robertson's Prophecy on 2020 U.S. Presidential Election Results & The Aftermath. (2020, October 20). [Video]. YouTube. https://www.youtube.com/watch?v=dF5izJ9KCug&t=107s

[xxxiv] RWW News: God Told Kat Kerr The Results Of The Next Five Presidential Elections. (2018b, February 23). [Video]. YouTube. https://www.youtube.com/watch?v=WRlldqlbK88

[xxxv] God showed me 3 types of people as Trump begins 2nd term. (2021, January 9). [Video]. YouTube. https://www.youtube.com/watch?v=t5BLpQ-sBBQ&t=21s

[xxxvi] Grenholm, M. (2020, November 16). *The Five Most Embarrassing Evangelical Reactions to the Election Results.* PCPJ. https://pcpj.org/2020/11/14/the-five-most-embarrassing-evangelical-reactions-to-the-election-results/

[xxxvii] *Kim Clement Prophecy | The Trump Prophecies, ISIS, Socialism, Russia, China.* (2018, September 27). [Video]. YouTube. https://www.youtube.com/watch?v=VlXfkO3PWhA&t=906s

[xxxviii] *Trump Prophecies 2020, Impeachment. Two term president.* (2020, March 9). [Video]. YouTube. https://www.youtube.com/watch?v=X1gCNlO-Jsc&t=716s

[xxxix] ibid

[xl] *Trump 2020 Prophecy - Kim Clement.* (2019, December 19). [Video]. YouTube. https://www.youtube.com/watch?v=9w8Mr0kylwc&t=159s

www.ingramcontent.com/pod-product-compliance
Lightning Source LLC
Chambersburg PA
CBHW071936020426
42331CB00010B/2899